THE
FUTURE IS
UNITED

INTO 2000 AND BEYOND WITH
MANCHESTER UNITED

SAM PILGER

Designer Dominic Zwemmer
Editors Karen Dolan, Jill Somerscales
Picture Researcher Dominic Zwemmer
Editorial Director Christiane Gunzi

First published in Great Britain in 1999 by
Manchester United Books, an imprint of
André Deutsch Ltd
76 Dean Street, London W1V 5HA (www.vci.co.uk)
Produced by **Picthall & Gunzi Ltd** for André Deutsch Ltd

Reproduction in England by Digicol.
Printed and bound in Italy.

CIP data for this title is available from the British Library.

ISBN 0233 99829 2

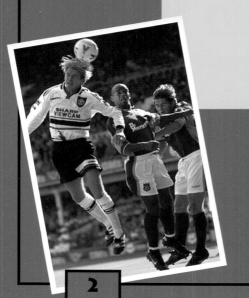

CONTENTS

In 1999 Manchester United became the first-ever English team to win the European Cup, FA Cup and Premiership title in the same season. This great side has made football history and will never be forgotten, especially by their devoted fans.

LEAGUE CHAMPS

Manchester United won their fifth Premiership title in seven seasons, when Cole (seen here against Derby County), and Beckham scored to beat Tottenham Hotspur 2-1 on the season's final day.

FA. B!

Solskjaer scored the winner against Liverpool in Round 4 as United became FA Cup winners for a record tenth time. They beat Newcastle 2-0 at Wembley, with goals from Sheringham and Scholes.

EUROPEAN KINGS

On the way to the European final, Dwight Yorke scored as United beat Brondby 5-0. Last-minute goals from Sheringham and Solskjaer won United the European Cup in a 2-1 victory over Bayern Munich in Barcelona.

PREMIERSHIP CHAMPIONS 1998/99

FA CUP WINNERS 1998/99

EUROPEAN CHAMPIONS LEAGUE WINNERS 1998/99

CENTURY

Superstars
Manchester United scored an amazing 128 goals and lost only four games during the greatest season in their history!

5

THE SEASON STARTS

In the summer of 1998, United spent £28 million on new players, trying to catch up with Arsenal, who were top of the League. But in United's first League game against Arsenal, they lost 0-3! Just four days later, United began to get back on a winning track by beating their old rivals, Liverpool, 2-0 at Old Trafford. This shows United's team spirit and powers of recovery.

GUNNERS UP

Tony Adams scored first for Arsenal with a header and Nicolas Anelka scored with a ball into an empty net after Schmeichel had saved Anelka's first try. Then Arsenal's new player Ljungberg lobbed in a ball to finish 3-0 up.

FA CARLING PREMIERSHIP

20TH SEPTEMBER, 1998

ARSENAL 3 MANCHESTER UNITED 0

And that's a fact!

United's manager, Sir Alex Ferguson, said "This game is one I want to forget. Arsenal were more determined, while we were always second best."

LIVERPOOL LICKED!

Andy Cole leaps over Stig Inge Bjornebye during United's 2-0 win over Liverpool. Denis Irwin gave United the lead from the penalty spot, then Paul Scholes smashed in a second goal to settle the game, with ten minutes to go.

FA CARLING PREMIERSHIP

24TH SEPTEMBER, 1998

MANCHESTER UNITED 2 LIVERPOOL 0

Free Kicks
Denis Irwin is an ace taker of free kicks, but since David Beckham started playing for Manchester United, Denis hasn't had a look-in!

"It doesn't bother me that I don't get the same attention as Giggs and Becks. I like it this way, I just get on with playing football."
Denis Irwin

DENIS IRWIN

ALL ABOUT DENIS

Denis Irwin has won 10 medals at Manchester United, making him and Peter Schmeichel the most successful players in the club's history.

POSITION: DEFENDER
BORN: CORK, IRELAND
DATE OF BIRTH: 31.10.1965
HEIGHT: 5 FEET 8 INCHES
WEIGHT: 10 ST 8 LB
JOINED UNITED: 8.6.1990
COST UNITED: £625,000
FIRST GAME: V COVENTRY CITY 25.8.1990
PLAYED FOR UNITED: 415
PREMIER LEAGUE GOALS: 19
FA CUP GOALS: 3
LEAGUE CUP GOALS: 0
EUROPE GOALS: 6
TOTAL UNITED GOALS: 28
PLAYED FOR IRELAND: 52
GOALS FOR IRELAND: 4

THE PERFECT PAIR

This game showed United at their very best. They scored five times, hit the post twice and made many more attempts to get goals. If Wimbledon's goalkeeper, Neil Sullivan, had not been on such great form, United might even have beaten their Premiership record of nine goals against Ipswich three years earlier.

VERY KEANE

Roy Keane missed most of the previous season with a knee injury. In the game against Wimbledon, he ruled midfield, and showed he was back on top form. Here he runs at Wimbledon's Kenny Cunningham.

And that's a fact!

Before Roy Keane became a professional footballer, he used to be an amateur boxer in Ireland. He had four fights and won all of them!

TWO AS ONE

Cole and Yorke showed off their amazing partnership after only three games together. They are also very good friends off the pitch.

FA CARLING PREMIERSHIP
17TH OCTOBER, 1998
MANCHESTER UNITED 5 WIMBLEDON 1

ALL ABOUT ROY

Roy Keane takes his place as one of the finest footballers and captains in United's history. In 1997 Roy was voted Britain's top player by readers of *Match of the Day* magazine.

POSITION: MIDFIELDER
BORN: CORK, IRELAND
DATE OF BIRTH: 10.8.1971
HEIGHT: 5 FEET 10 INCHES
WEIGHT: 11ST 3LB
SIGNED FOR UNITED: 19.7.93
COST UNITED: £3.75 MILLION
FIRST GAME: V NORWICH CITY 15.8.1993
PLAYED FOR UNITED: 215
PREMIER LEAGUE GOALS: 19
FA CUP GOALS: 1
LEAGUE CUP GOALS: 0
EUROPE GOALS: 6
TOTAL UNITED GOALS: 26
PLAYED FOR IRELAND: 42
GOALS FOR IRELAND: 5

Goodness!
As a child, Roy Keane wrote to every top English club except United because he didn't think he was good enough for them!

ROY KEANE

BRONDBY'S BEATEN

Sir Alex Ferguson describes United's 5-0 victory against Brondby as one of the best displays that he has ever seen in his 12 years at Old Trafford.

By the 28th minute the contest was over. United had already scored four goals – one each from Beckham, Phil Neville, Cole and Yorke. Then, in the second half, Scholes scored a fifth!

DWIGHT ON, ANDY!

Cole worked with Yorke (pictured here) to cut through the Brondby defence, then finished off by chipping over the goalkeeper. Schmeichel called it the greatest goal he had ever seen at Old Trafford.

And that's a fact!

This 5-0 win meant that United had scored more goals in the Champions League group stage than ever before, and they still had two games to play.

UEFA CHAMPIONS LEAGUE – GROUP D

4TH NOVEMBER, 1998

MANCHESTER UNITED 5 BRONDBY 0

Not Cricket!
Neville could have played cricket for England but decided to stick with football. He broke batting records at youth level for Lancashire.

OLE'S OMEN

Phil Neville scored his second- ever goal for United in the 5-0 victory over Brondby. He scored his first goal in February 1998 against Chelsea. Before the game, his team mate Ole Gunnar had a strong feeling that Phil would score!

ALL ABOUT PHIL

Phil Neville can perform just as well at left-back or in midfield. Last season, he was often a substitute.

POSITION: DEFENDER/ MIDFIELDER
BORN: BURY, ENGLAND
DATE OF BIRTH: 21.1.1977
HEIGHT: 5 FEET 10 INCHES
WEIGHT: 11ST 10LB
JOINED UNITED: 5.7.93
FIRST GAME: V WREXHAM 28.1 .95
PLAYED FOR UNITED: 111
PREMIER LEAGUE GOALS: 1
FA CUP GOALS: 0
LEAGUE GUP GOALS: 0
EUROPE GOALS: 1
TOTAL UNITED GOALS: 2
GAMES FOR ENGLAND: 17
GOALS FOR ENGLAND: 0

"I would rather play 30 games a season for United than 80 games for anyone else. This is the only club to be at."

Phil Neville

Dwight Yorke walked into Old Trafford with his famous wide smile, and kept on smiling as he enjoyed a dream season, winning three medals and scoring 29 goals. Two of those goals came in the thrilling 3-3 draw with Barcelona in the Nou Camp. "Yorke has been just sensational," said Sir Alex Ferguson, "He's fitted in right away and enjoyed every minute of it."

ALL ABOUT DWIGHT

Dwight Yorke finished his first season at United as the Premiership's joint top goal scorer with 18 goals and joint top scorer in the Champions League with eight goals.

POSITION: FORWARD
BORN: TOBAGO
DATE OF BIRTH: 3.11.1971
HEIGHT: 5 FEET 10 INCHES
WEIGHT: 12 ST 4 LB
SIGNED FOR UNITED: 20.8.1998
COST UNITED: £12.6 MILLION
FIRST GAME: V WEST HAM UNITED 22.8.1998
PLAYED FOR UNITED: 48
PREMIER LEAGUE GOALS: 18
FA CUP GOALS: 3
LEAGUE CUP GOALS: 0
EUROPE GOALS: 8
TOTAL UNITED GOALS: 29
PLAYED FOR TRINIDAD AND TOBAGO: 40

Sideways Move
When Yorke was growing up in Tobago he used to catch crabs and sell them to restaurants, so that he could afford to buy football boots.

UEFA CHAMPIONS LEAGUE – GROUP D
25TH NOVEMBER, 1998
BARCELONA 3 MANCHESTER UNITED 3

"I don't think people realised how good a player Dwight was until he came to United."

Ryan Giggs

DWIGHT YORKE

IN SAFE HANDS!

In his eight seasons at Old Trafford, Peter Schmeichel proved himself to be one of the greatest goalkeepers ever. His list of honours at United included five Premiership titles, three FA Cups, the League Cup and the European Cup.

In his last season at United he lost a little of his usual sparkling form, but he came back at his very best as United won the Treble. It seemed right that the Dane ended his United career by becoming only the second player ever to captain Manchester United to the European Cup, after the dramatic win over Bayern Munich in Spain.

SAVING THE DAY

Schmeichel saved United's season when he turned away Bergkamp's penalty in the last minute of the FA Cup semi-final replay against Arsenal.

HEAD OVER HEELS

Schmeichel cartwheeled for joy across his goal mouth when he realised that Solskjaer's goal had won them the European Cup and the Treble!

"Leaving United hurt me, but it was something I had to do. I want to go on for as long as I can, so I need to play on the continent."

Peter Schmeichel

PETER SCHMEICHEL

Great Dane!
In 170 games for United, Schmeichel has let in only 132 goals and in 95 games no goals got past him at all !

THE GREAT ESCAPE

In the fourth round of the FA Cup, against Liverpool at Old Trafford, Michael Owen gave Liverpool the lead after only three minutes. For most of the game it looked as though Liverpool were going to beat their old rivals in the FA Cup for the first time in 78 years.

Time was running out, but United never gave up hope, and in the 88th minute Dwight Yorke equalised. Two minutes later Ole Gunnar Solskjaer scored the winner!

ALL DWIGHT!
From a Beckham free kick, Cole crossed for Dwight Yorke to score from close range to make it 1-1.

DREAM BOY!
Ole Gunnar Solskjaer had always dreamt that one day he might score the winning goal against Liverpool, the team he supported as a young boy.

And that's a fact!
Sir Alex Ferguson joked that United were not really interested in the FA Cup. No one was fooled for a moment, though!

FA CUP FOURTH ROUND
24ᵀᴴ JANUARY, 1999
MANCHESTER UNITED 2 LIVERPOOL 1

"Everything about Jaap Stam is absolutely first class. We know we are going to get several years of sterling work from him."

Sir Alex Ferguson

Mega Money
Jaap Stam moved from PSV Eindhoven to United in 1998 for £10.75 million! This was a world record fee for a defender.

ALL ABOUT JAAP

The costly Jaap Stam has not let United fans down. His speed, strength and skill are very important to the team's success.

POSITION: DEFENDER
BORN: HOLLAND
DATE OF BIRTH: 17.7.1972
HEIGHT: 6 FEET 3 INCHES
WEIGHT: 13 ST 9 LB
JOINED UNITED: 1.7.1998
COST UNITED: £10.75 MILLION
FIRST GAME: V LKS LODZ (POLAND) CHAMPIONS LEAGUE Q2 12.8.1999
PLAYED FOR UNITED: 49
PREMIER LEAGUE GOALS: 1
FA CUP GOALS: 0
LEAGUE CUP GOALS: 0
EUROPE GOALS: 0
TOTAL UNITED GOALS: 1
PLAYED FOR HOLLAND: 25
GOALS FOR HOLLAND: 2

JAAP STAM

HIT FOR EIGHT

Ole Gunnar Solskjaer made history when he became the first substitute to get four goals in a match, as United scored a record 8-1 win against Nottingham Forest.

Ole replaced Dwight Yorke after 72 minutes, with United 4-1 up, and just 18 minutes later he had doubled United's score all on his own with two tap-ins, a volley and a long-range shot. Earlier, Cole and Yorke had scored two goals each, enough to knock Forest out of the game.

RECORD BREAKERS

This was Manchester United's biggest ever win away from home, beating their previous record of February 1970, when they recorded an 8-2 victory over Northampton Town.

FA CARLING PREMIERSHIP

6TH FEBRUARY, 1999

NOTTINGHAM FOREST 1 MANCHESTER UNITED 8

Ole Notspur!
Ole Gunnar could have been playing for Spurs last season after United accepted a bid of £5.5 million for him, but Ole wanted to stay at United.

FOREST FELLED

Nottingham Forest's manager, Ron Atkinson, said it was a good job United didn't bring Solskjaer on earlier! A very proud Sir Alex Ferguson praised his players by saying they displayed the best finishing he had seen at his time at United and that the team had never been stronger.

"I'm proud of my place in the record books. I'll always remember those 15 minutes. I wanted to get as many goals as I could."
Ole Gunnar Solskjaer

And that's a fact!
Ole Gunnar Solskjaer performed this amazing display in a pair of football boots he bought from his local sports shop the day before the match.

INTER BATTLE

United proved they could win the European Cup after they beat Inter Milan's superstars. United's own stars, Beckham and Yorke, worked together to give United a two-goal advantage in the Champions League quarter-final. In the San Siro stadium, Ventola scored for Inter Milan after 63 minutes. Scholes scored with two minutes to go and United were through to the semi-finals.

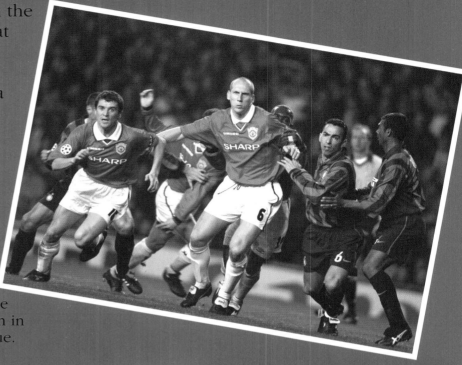

MY BALL!

Roy Keane and Jaap Stam battle for the ball with Youri Djorkaeff of Inter Milan in the first game of the Champions League.

YORKE STRIKES

After six minutes Beckham lobbed in a ball which Yorke guided into the net with a diving header. Then Beckham crossed again, for Yorke to head in a second goal. United only drew with Barcelona and Bayern Munich in the group stages, but now they had proved they could beat the best.

And that's a fact!

After the World Cup incident, Beckham made up with Inter Milan's midfielder Diego Simeone by swapping shirts. It was his Mum's idea!

UEFA CHAMPIONS LEAGUE QUARTER-FINAL

3RD MARCH, 1999

MANCHESTER UNITED 2 INTER MILAN 0

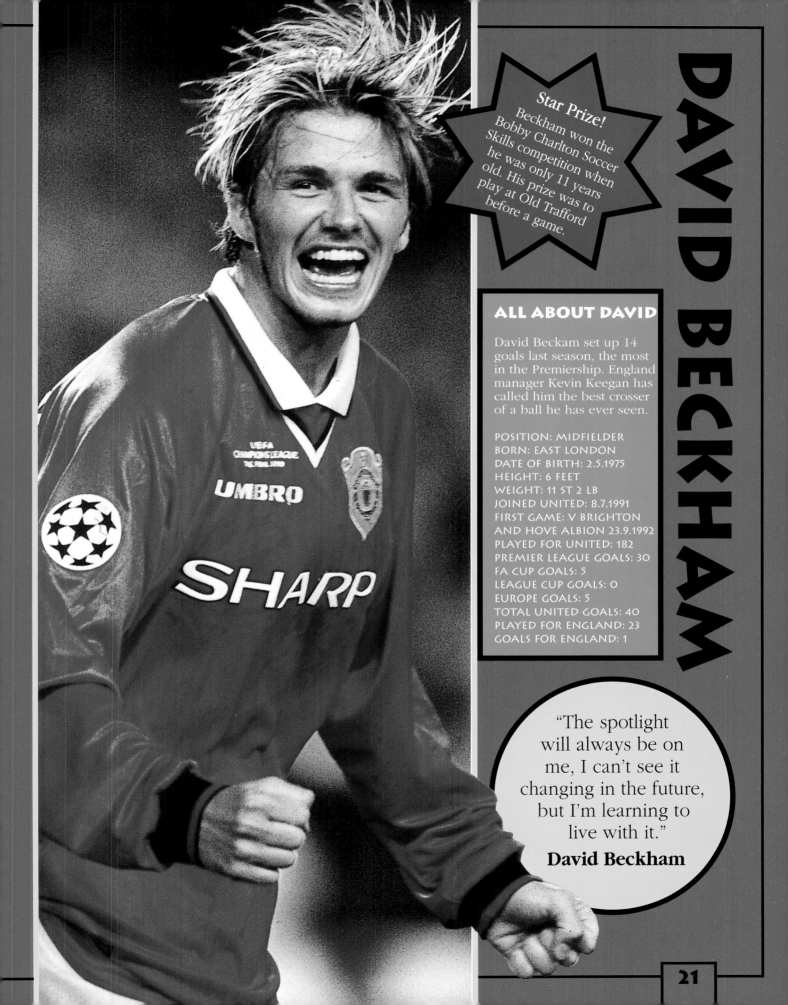

DAVID BECKHAM

ALL ABOUT DAVID

David Beckam set up 14 goals last season, the most in the Premiership. England manager Kevin Keegan has called him the best crosser of a ball he has ever seen.

POSITION: MIDFIELDER
BORN: EAST LONDON
DATE OF BIRTH: 2.5.1975
HEIGHT: 6 FEET
WEIGHT: 11 ST 2 LB
JOINED UNITED: 8.7.1991
FIRST GAME: V BRIGHTON
AND HOVE ALBION 23.9.1992
PLAYED FOR UNITED: 182
PREMIER LEAGUE GOALS: 30
FA CUP GOALS: 5
LEAGUE CUP GOALS: 0
EUROPE GOALS: 5
TOTAL UNITED GOALS: 40
PLAYED FOR ENGLAND: 23
GOALS FOR ENGLAND: 1

"The spotlight will always be on me, I can't see it changing in the future, but I'm learning to live with it."
David Beckham

21

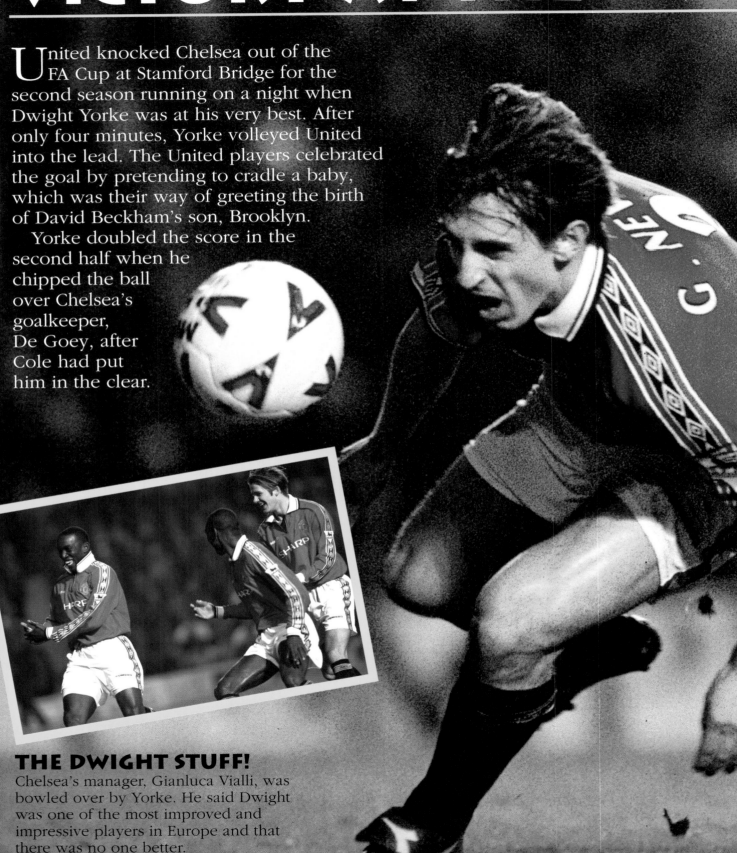

VICTORY AT THE BRI

United knocked Chelsea out of the FA Cup at Stamford Bridge for the second season running on a night when Dwight Yorke was at his very best. After only four minutes, Yorke volleyed United into the lead. The United players celebrated the goal by pretending to cradle a baby, which was their way of greeting the birth of David Beckham's son, Brooklyn.

Yorke doubled the score in the second half when he chipped the ball over Chelsea's goalkeeper, De Goey, after Cole had put him in the clear.

THE DWIGHT STUFF!

Chelsea's manager, Gianluca Vialli, was bowled over by Yorke. He said Dwight was one of the most improved and impressive players in Europe and that there was no one better.

BOOKED!

Gary and his brother, Phil, became the first Manchester United players to write a diary of a season at the club with their book *For Club and Country*.

ALL ABOUT GARY

Gary Neville's performance last season proved that he is an international-class defender. One day he may be captain of Manchester United and England.

POSITION: DEFENDER
BORN: BURY, LANCASHIRE
DATE OF BIRTH: 18.2.1975
HEIGHT: 5 FEET 10 INCHES
WEIGHT: 11 ST 11 LB
JOINED UNITED: 8.7.1991
FIRST GAME: V TOPEDO MOSCOW 16.9.1992
PLAYED FOR UNITED: 202
PREMIER LEAGUE GOALS: 2
FA CUP GOALS: 0
LEAGUE CUP GOALS: 0
EUROPE GOALS: 0
TOTAL UNITED GOALS: 2
PLAYED FOR ENGLAND: 32
GOALS FOR ENGLAND: 0

And that's a fact!

When Gary Neville first played for England he had played only 19 league games. This is the lowest number ever for an England player.

"It actually meant something when we won the European Cup. It affected people's lives. We were out of control with delight."

Gary Neville

FA CUP SIXTH ROUND REPLAY
10TH MARCH, 1999
CHELSEA 0 MANCHESTER UNITED 2

Many people think this thrilling game was the greatest ever, when United beat Arsenal to make it to the FA Cup final. The game lasted 120 minutes and swung between the two teams. First United then Arsenal thought they were on their way to Wembley. Beckham gave United the lead in the first half with a wonderful goal, but Arsenal clawed their way back when Denis Bergkamp scored. The London players were also helped when Roy Keane was sent off, but United won the game in extra time with a brilliant goal from Giggs.

Fans-tastic!
After the final whistle Manchester United fans invaded the pitch, lifted David Beckham on to their shoulders and carried him off!

SHARP SHOT

From a pass by Teddy Sheringham in the 17th minute, David Beckham hit a super shot from 20 yards. The ball curled away from Arsenal goalkeeper David Seaman and into the net, to put Manchester United 1-0 up in the game.

STAM'S THE MAN!

Jaap Stam dives in to steal the ball from Arsenal's Nicolas Anelka. Anelka thought he had won the game for Arsenal in the second half, but his goal was ruled offside.

And that's a fact!

After 118 years, this was the last-ever FA Cup semi-final replay. Semi finals will now be decided in one game, with extra time and penalties.

"Everybody was ecstatic after the game. We showed what a great team spirit we have. Winning trophies is in our blood."

Sir Alex Ferguson

FA CUP SEMI-FINAL REPLAY
14TH APRIL, 1999
ARSENAL 1 MANCHESTER UNITED 2

Ryan Giggs scored what is probably the greatest goal of all time to win the FA Cup semi-final replay at Villa Park. With only 10 men on the pitch, United were under constant pressure in extra time, before Giggs' genius goal settled the tie.

In the second half of extra time, Giggs picked up a stray pass from Arsenal's Patrick Vieira in his own half and set off towards the goal. He beat Vieira, weaved past Martin Keown twice, then passed Dixon on the edge of the area, before beating Tony Adams to the ball and blasting a shot over Seaman.

Wish List
"I would love to have scored that one. It was one of the great goals of modern football."

Diego Maradona

"You don't realise what kind of goal it is on the pitch, I just went for it. It's incredible that people are saying it was one of the best goals ever scored."

Ryan Giggs

EXTRA SPECIAL

Giggs' amazing goal was made even more special by the fact that Arsenal had the best defensive record in the whole of Europe in the 1998/99 season.

ALL ABOUT RYAN

Ryan Giggs plays his international football for Wales. He also captained England schoolboys when he was 15 years old.

POSITION: FORWARD
BORN: CARDIFF, WALES
DATE OF BIRTH: 29.11.1973
HEIGHT: 5 FEET 11 INCHES
WEIGHT: 10 ST 7LB
JOINED UNITED: 9.7.1990
FIRST GAME: V EVERTON 2.3.1991
PLAYED FOR UNITED: 319
PREMIER LEAGUE GOALS: 53
FA CUP GOALS: 7
LEAGUE CUP GOALS: 6
EUROPE GOALS: 10
TOTAL UNITED GOALS: 76
PLAYED FOR WALES: 24
GOALS FOR WALES: 5

THE ITALIAN JOB

Manchester United booked their place in the European Cup final with an amazing comeback against their old Italian rivals, Juventus. The first game at Old Trafford ended 1-1 after Ryan Giggs had rescued United with a last-minute equaliser. But 10 minutes into the second leg in Turin, Juventus had a two-goal lead, thanks to Filipo Inzaghi. The first goal was a tap-in, and the second was a lucky deflection off Jaap Stam. It looked as though United would miss out on the final yet again.

KEANE HOPE

Beckham jumps over a challenge from Ciro Ferrara of Juventus. It was from Beckham's superb corner that Roy Keane headed United back into the game in the 24th minute.

Numero Uno!
This was United's first-ever win in Italy. They had previously failed on seven occasions, four times to Juventus, twice to AC Milan and once to Inter Milan.

And that's a fact!
Sadly, bookings for Roy Keane and Paul Scholes meant that they would not be able to play in the European Cup final in May.

UEFA CHAMPIONS LEAGUE SEMI-FINAL

21ST APRIL, 1999

JUVENTUS 2 MANCHESTER UNITED 3

YORKE HEADS FOR GLORY

Dwight Yorke made the score 2-2 before half time, when he met Andy Cole's cross with a spectacular diving header. If the result stayed the same, United were through, as they had now scored more goals away from home.

"That victory in Turin gave me the most pleasure. The first half was the best ever football United have played for me."
Sir Alex Ferguson

KING COLE

A 2-2 draw would have been enough, but Andy Cole tapped in the winner with four minutes to go, to make the score 3-2. This put United in the European Cup final for the first time since 1968, 31 years ago.

PREMIER CHAMPS

COLE CONTROL

Andy Cole came on as a substitute for the second half and, with his first two touches of the ball, he scored the goal that made United champions. Gary Neville played a long ball forward, Cole controlled it, then lobbed it over Ian Walker. United were champions!

On the last day of the season, Manchester United won their fifth Premiership title in seven years with a 2-1 victory over Tottenham Hotspur. This title meant a lot to Alex Ferguson, as it was the first time United had won the title at Old Trafford. He called it "a dream I've cherished for 13 years." It wasn't easy for United to begin with, as they went behind to a Les Ferdinand goal in the first half.

BECK'S BACK

Beckham relieved the tension when he equalised for United on the stroke of half time, blasting in a pass from Scholes.

FA CARLING PREMIERSHIP

16TH MAY, 1999

MANCHESTER UNITED 2 TOTTENHAM HOTSPUR 1

ALL ABOUT ANDY

Andy Cole still holds the record for scoring the most goals in a Premiership season. He got 34 for Newcastle in 1993/94.

POSITION: FORWARD
BORN: NOTTINGHAM
DATE OF BIRTH: 15.10.1971
HEIGHT: 5 FEET 11 INCHES
WEIGHT: 11 ST 2 LB
JOINED UNITED: 12.1.1995
COST UNITED: £6.25 MILLION
AND PLAYER EXCHANGE
FIRST GAME: V BLACKBURN
ROVERS 22.1.1995
PLAYED FOR UNITED : 155
PREMIER LEAGUE GOALS: 61
FA CUP GOALS: 9
LEAGUE CUP GOALS: 0
EUROPE GOALS: 11
TOTAL UNITED GOALS: 81
PLAYED FOR ENGLAND: 5
GOALS FOR ENGLAND: 0

"I was overjoyed when Dwight Yorke arrived. I get on so well with him. If he needs anything, I'm there for him."
Andy Cole

FA CUP WINNERS

Manchester United completed their third double in six seasons by beating Newcastle 2-0 in the FA Cup final. It didn't look good for United when their captain, Roy Keane, hobbled off with an injury after only six minutes, but moments later his replacement, Teddy Sheringham put United into the lead after he had played a one-two with Paul Scholes. "We were beaten by the better team. They have to be one of the best of all time," said Newcastle captain, Alan Shearer.

EASY!
Newcastle were simply not good enough to worry United. David May said he couldn't believe how easy it was! United settled the contest after 53 minutes when Sheringham passed to Scholes, who put a low shot into the net.

FA CUP FINAL
22ND MAY, 1999
MANCHESTER UNITED 2 NEWCASTLE UNITED 0

> "There isn't another player like him in the whole world. Scholesy is just about the complete player."
>
> **Glenn Hoddle**

ALL ABOUT PAUL

Sir Alex thinks Scholes is the best passer at United, Gary Neville believes he is the best tackler, and Phil Neville says he is the best finisher.

POSITION:
MIDFIELDER/FORWARD
BORN: SALFORD, ENGLAND
DATE OF BIRTH: 16.11.1974
HEIGHT: 5 FEET 7 INCHES
WEIGHT: 11 ST 8 LB
JOINED UNITED: 8.7.1991
FIRST GAME: V PORT VALE 21.9.1994
PLAYED FOR UNITED: 121
PREMIER LEAGUE GOALS: 32
FA CUP GOALS: 4
LEAGUE CUP GOALS: 5
EUROPE GOALS: 7
TOTAL UNITED GOALS: 48
PLAYED FOR ENGLAND: 17
GOALS FOR ENGLAND: 7

WE WON THE CUP!

United's goal scorers, Teddy Sheringham and Paul Scholes, hold up the trophy after Manchester United had won the FA Cup for a record 10th time. Each player had set up a goal for the other to score in the 2-0 win.

Junior Scholes
Paul became a dad in July 1999 when his wife Claire gave birth to a baby boy called Aaron Jake.

KINGS OF EUROPE

On a glorious night in Barcelona, Spain, United came back from nearly losing against Bayern Munich to become the champions of Europe.

They started the game nervously and went a goal behind after only six minutes, when the midfielder Mario Basler curled a free-kick past Schmeichel. When the clock showed 90 minutes had been played, it looked as if United had lost. Then they got one last chance and won a corner one minute into injury time!

READY TEDDY GO!

Peter Schmeichel came up for the corner. This confused the Germans, and they did not clear the ball away from the goal properly. Ryan Giggs shot the ball back and Teddy Sheringham was there to put it in the net and save United!

OLE'S BIG MOMENT

Soon, United won another corner. David Beckham raced over to take it and swung in a cross for Teddy Sheringham. Sheringham headed it on towards Ole Gunnar Solskjaer, who managed to score with his toe. This goal is Ole's most famous moment. United went from defeat to victory in less than two minutes!

CHAMPIONS LEAGUE FINAL
26TH JUNE, 1999
MANCHESTER UNITED 2 BAYERN MUNICH 1

And that's a fact!
Bayern Munich's ribbons were already being put on the European Cup when United scored their two goals. The ribbons had to be changed quickly!

ALL ABOUT OLE

In the 1998/99 season, Ole scored a goal more often than any other player in the Premiership. He scored about every 71 minutes that he was on the pitch!

POSITION: FORWARD
BORN: NORWAY
DATE OF BIRTH: 26.2.1973
HEIGHT: 5 FEET 9 INCHES
WEIGHT: 11 ST 10 LB
JOINED UNITED: 29.7.1996
COST UNITED: £1.5 MILLION
FIRST GAME: V BLACKBURN
ROVERS 25.8.1996
PLAYED FOR UNITED: 112
PREMIER LEAGUE GOALS: 36
FA CUP GOALS: 3
LEAGUE CUP GOALS: 3
EUROPE GOALS: 4
TOTAL UNITED GOALS: 46
PLAYED FOR NORWAY: 21
GOALS FOR NORWAY: 10

"Now you know why I have stayed with United. I have never had a better feeling than when that goal went in and I doubt I ever will."

Ole Gunnar Solskjaer

TREBLE WINNER!

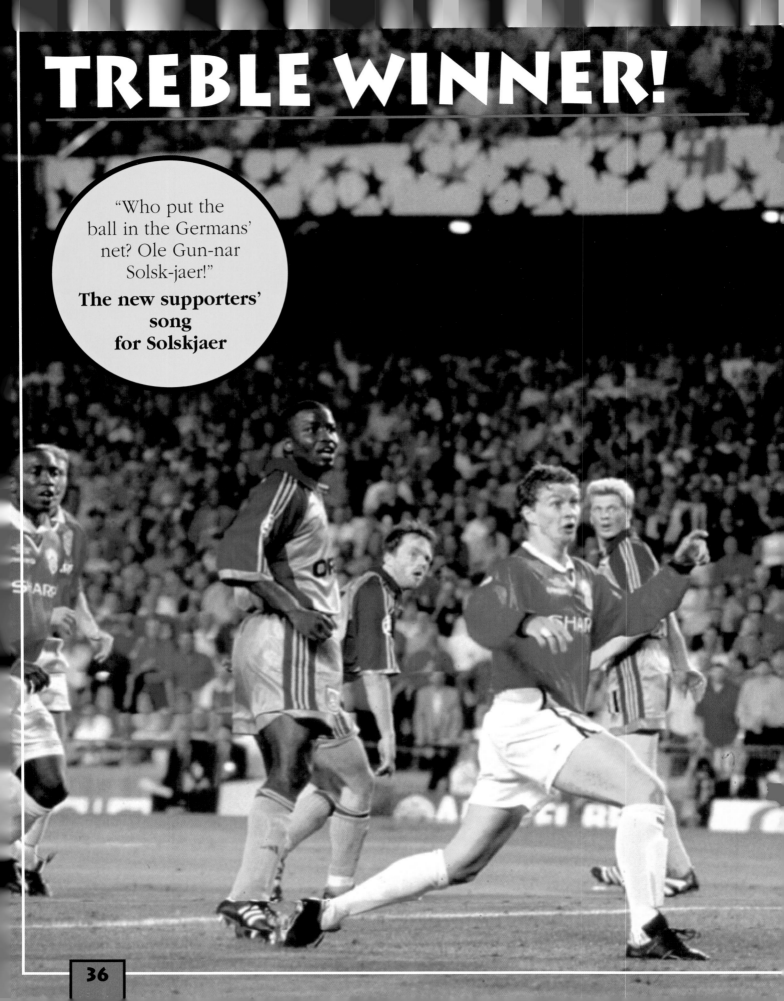

"Who put the ball in the Germans' net? Ole Gun-nar Solsk-jaer!"

The new supporters' song for Solskjaer

TREBLE DECKERS

On the day after United's dramatic European Cup win, 750,000 people took to the streets of Manchester to welcome their heroes home from Barcelona. Fans hung from traffic lights, stood on top of bus shelters and clambered on to scaffolding to catch a glimpse of the Manchester United squad parading the European Cup, the FA Cup and the Premiership trophy from the top of an open bus. The bus slowly made its way to the *Manchester Evening News* Arena where it was greeted by 17,000 fans.

Special Bus
The number on the front of the bus was changed to 2-1 to celebrate the score of United's victory over Bayern Munich the night before.

ON STAGE

At the celebration in the Arena, each player went up on to the stage in turn and lifted the European Cup to a deafening roar from the excited crowd. Sir Alex Ferguson gave a speech, thanking all the fans for their support.

And that's a fact!
One fan held up a card that read: "Man United – the microwave champs. Two minutes from stone cold to well-cooked."

38

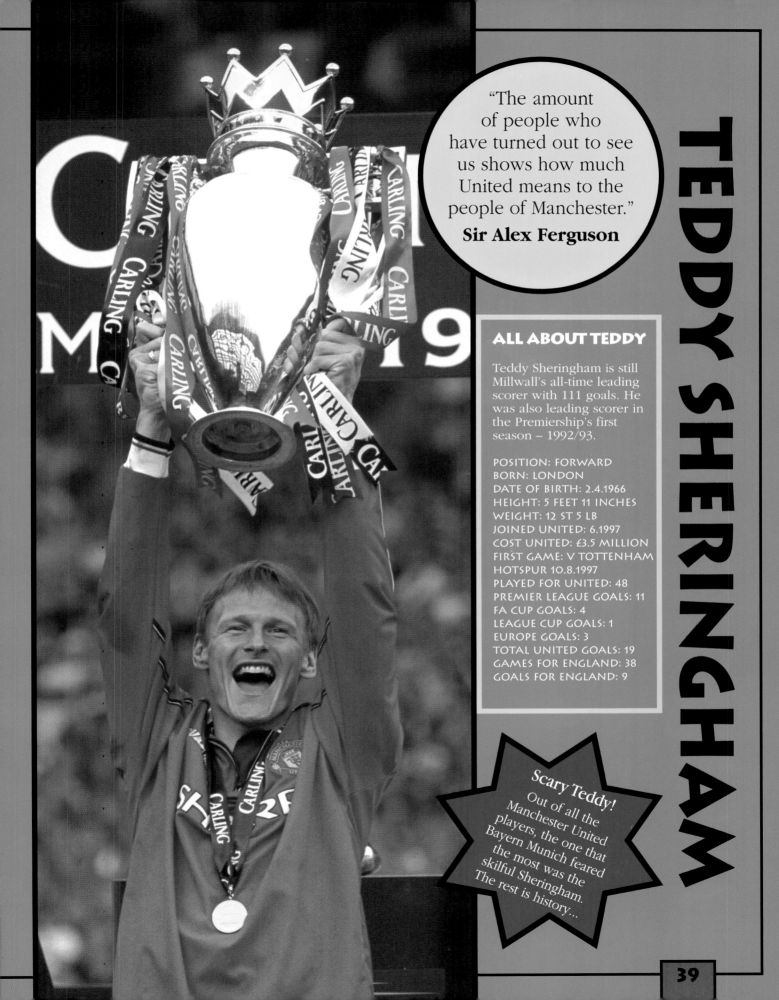

> "The amount of people who have turned out to see us shows how much United means to the people of Manchester."
> **Sir Alex Ferguson**

ALL ABOUT TEDDY

Teddy Sheringham is still Millwall's all-time leading scorer with 111 goals. He was also leading scorer in the Premiership's first season – 1992/93.

POSITION: FORWARD
BORN: LONDON
DATE OF BIRTH: 2.4.1966
HEIGHT: 5 FEET 11 INCHES
WEIGHT: 12 ST 5 LB
JOINED UNITED: 6.1997
COST UNITED: £3.5 MILLION
FIRST GAME: V TOTTENHAM
HOTSPUR 10.8.1997
PLAYED FOR UNITED: 48
PREMIER LEAGUE GOALS: 11
FA CUP GOALS: 4
LEAGUE CUP GOALS: 1
EUROPE GOALS: 3
TOTAL UNITED GOALS: 19
GAMES FOR ENGLAND: 38
GOALS FOR ENGLAND: 9

Scary Teddy!
Out of all the Manchester United players, the one that Bayern Munich feared the most was the skilful Sheringham. The rest is history...

FUTURE FACES

The stream of young talent at United shows no sign of stopping. The youth system that has given the team Beckham, Butt, Scholes, Giggs and the Neville brothers has more youngsters ready to become stars in the new millennium. Sir Alex has already said that Wes Brown will most likely become Jaap Stam's defensive partner, when he has recovered from his knee injury.

COACH AND TROPHIES

Not many people had heard of Steve McClaren when Sir Alex Ferguson brought him from Derby County to Old Trafford to be his assistant manager in February 1999. Still, by the end of the season he had coached United to three major trophies and had not lost a single game.

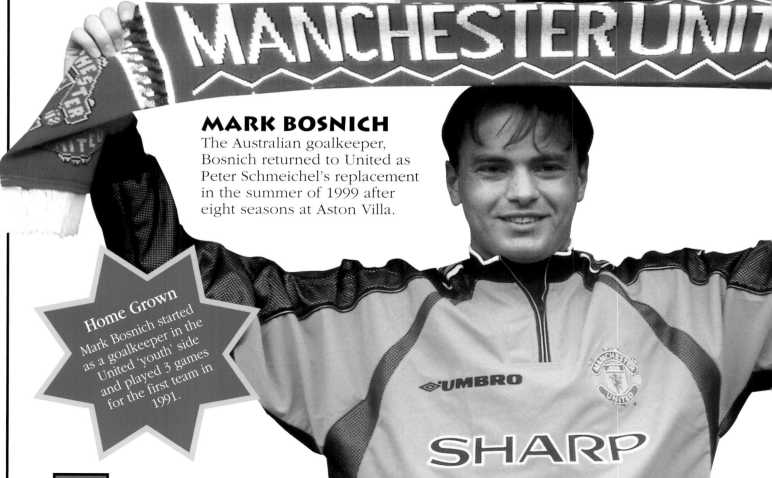

MARK BOSNICH

The Australian goalkeeper, Bosnich returned to United as Peter Schmeichel's replacement in the summer of 1999 after eight seasons at Aston Villa.

Home Grown
Mark Bosnich started as a goalkeeper in the United 'youth' side and played 3 games for the first team in 1991.

WES BROWN

The talented defender finished his first full season at United with both the Premiership and Champions League winners' medals.

> "If you're good enough, you're old enough. I've always believed that the player you produce is better than the player you buy."
>
> **Sir Alex Ferguson**

JONATHAN GREENING

Signed for £1 million from York City in March 1998, Greening has impressed Sir Alex Ferguson on the right side of midfield whenever he gets the chance.

ALEX NOTMAN

The young Scottish striker first played in the Worthington Cup before being loaned to Aberdeen.

MARK WILSON

Mark first played in the Champions League against Brondby last season, then starred in the Far East tour of summer 1999.

FOES OF THE FUTUR

Manchester United won the Treble in 1999, but there are plenty of great sides, at home and abroad, just waiting for a chance to topple them from the throne. United beat Arsenal in the 1999 Premiership title by only one point. When Arsenal won in 1998, it was also by a single point – too close for comfort!

DREAM TEAM

Sir Alex Ferguson's choice of the best eleven of non-United players in the Premiership included eight Arsenal players: Adams, Seaman, Keown, Petit, Bergkamp, Winterburn, Vieira and Overmars.

Huge-ventus!
Juventus are the Manchester United of Italy, with supporters' clubs all across the country. They have won the Italian championship 25 times.

MOMENT-US

Juventus have reached three Champions League Cup finals in the last four seasons. With players like Davids, Del Piero and Zidane, they will continue to be one of the very best teams in Europe.

SPAIN REIGN

Louis Van Gaal has created a wonderful squad of players at the Nou Camp, including Rivaldo, the De Boer brothers and Litmanen. Barcelona have won the Spanish championship for the past two seasons.

BARCELONA

GOLD TRAFFORD!

Manchester United are now expanding Old Trafford into a stadium fit for the new millennium.

The building work began in the summer of 1999 and it will be finished for the start of the 2001/02 season. Old Trafford will then regain its place as Britain's biggest football club stadium, with room for 67,400 people!

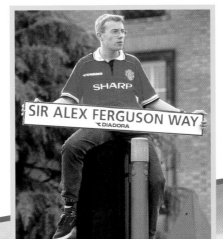

SURE SIGN

As this fan watches his heroes come home with the Treble, he shows that he thinks Alex Ferguson should be knighted, after such a record-breaking season.

Open Day

Old Trafford was opened on February 19th, 1910, when 45,000 people watched Liverpool beat Manchester United 4-3.

NEW HIGHS

An extra level costing £15 million will be added to the East and West stands behind the goals, bringing them up to the same height as the North stand. The East stand will be ready for the beginning of 2000/01.

ARISE, SIR ALEX!

Sir Alex was awarded a knighthood for his services to football on July 20th, 1999. When he was at Buckingham Palace, the Queen told him that she thought no team would ever win the Treble again.

"Most of my players, like Keane, Giggs, Cole and Beckham are still maturing... I think we've yet to see the best of them."

Sir Alex Ferguson

And that's a fact!

Sir Alex Ferguson plans to retire from football in 2002. He will be 60 years old and says he will need a rest!

SIR ALEX FERGUSON

ALL ABOUT ALEX

United players won't have to call Alex Ferguson 'Sir'. "I would never ask them to call me that," says Sir Alex, "they will continue to call me the boss or the gaffer."

HIS HONOURS AT MANCHESTER UNITED:

PREMIERSHIP WINNERS
1993, 1994, 1996, 1997, 1999
FA CUP WINNERS
1990, 1994, 1996, 1999
EUROPEAN CUP WINNERS
1999
EUROPEAN CUP WINNERS
CUP WINNERS 1991
LEAGUE CUP WINNERS 1992
EUROPEAN SUPER CUP
WINNERS 1991
CHARITY SHIELD WINNERS
1990, 1993, 1994, 1996, 1997

The summer after winning the Treble, Manchester United set out to take on the world. In the space of two weeks, they swept through Australia, China and Hong Kong, playing in front of 269,000 fans. Manchester United are like a pop group in the Far East, and wherever they went, they were met with huge crowds of screaming girls.

ALL WHITE!

United played the Australian Socceroos in Sydney's new stadium, built for the 2000 Olympics. They beat them 1-0, with Yorke scoring the winning goal. Jonathan Greening shows off United's new white training kit.

UPLIFTING!

Teddy Sheringham and Denis Irwin lift the trophy after beating the Socceroos twice. They played the first game at Melbourne Cricket Ground and won 2-0, with Jesper Blomqvist and Nicky Butt each scoring a brilliant goal.

OZ OUR SIDE!

Mark Bosnich returned home to Australia to a hero's welcome. In a country of cricket and rugby players, Bosnich is helping to make football more popular.

PRE-SEASON WORLD TOUR

AUSTRALIA 0 MANCHESTER UNITED 2

AUSTRALIA 0 MANCHESTER UNITED 1

SHANG HAI SHENHUA 0 MANCHESTER UNITED 2

SOUTH CHINA 0 MANCHESTER UNITED 2

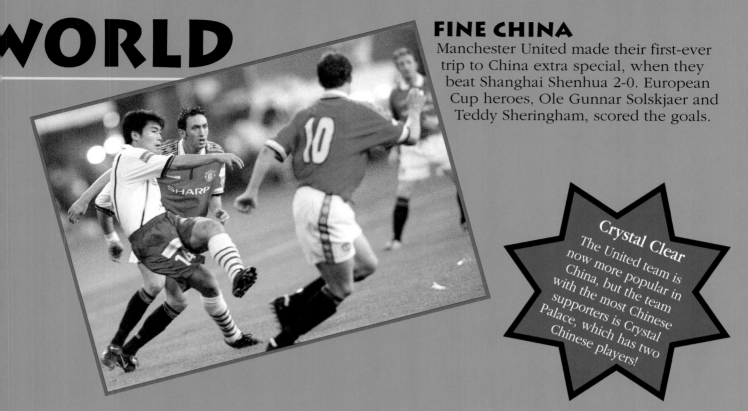

FINE CHINA

Manchester United made their first-ever trip to China extra special, when they beat Shanghai Shenhua 2-0. European Cup heroes, Ole Gunnar Solskjaer and Teddy Sheringham, scored the goals.

Crystal Clear

The United team is now more popular in China, but the team with the most Chinese supporters is Crystal Palace, which has two Chinese players!

UNITED LINE-UP FOR THE 1999/2000 SEASON

Back row: Wes Brown, Jordi Cruyff, David Beckham, Andy Cole, Nicky Butt, Dwight Yorke, Phil Neville, Ryan Giggs, Mark Wilson, David May, Gary Neville.

Middle row: Mike Stone (Doctor), Jimmy Curran (Physio's Aid), Albert Morgan (Kitman), Teddy Sheringham, Henning Berg, Rai van der Gouw, Mark Bosnich, Nick Culkin, Jaap Stam, Jonathan Greening, Jim Ryan (Reserve Team Manager), Tony Coton (Goalkeeper Coach), Rob Swire (Physio).

Front row: John Curtis, Jesper Blomqvist, Ole Gunnar Solskjaer, Sir Alex Ferguson (Manager), Roy Keane, Steve McClaren (Assistant Manager), Michael Clegg, Denis Irwin, Paul Scholes.

INDEX

PICTURE CREDITS
T=Top; M=Middle; B=Bottom; T/L=Top Left; T/R=Top Right; M/L=Middle Left; M/R=Middle Right; B/L=Bottom Left; B/R=Bottom Right;

Front Cover Popperfoto/Reuters
P.1 John Peters
P.2/3 John Peters
P.4/5 John Peters Popperfoto/Reuters B/R P.5
P.6/7 Allsport T/L and B/R P.6
John Peters P.7
P.8/9 Allsport
P10/11 Allsport M/L P.10
John Peters
P.12/13 Empics
P.14/15 Colorsport T/R P.14
Allsport P.14/15 and B/L P.15
P.16/17 John Peters B/L P.16
Allsport T/R P.16 and P.17
P.18/19 Allsport B/L P.18

Empics T/R P.18/19
P.20/21 John Peters T/R P.20
Empics B/L P.20
Allsport P21
P.22/23 John Peters B/R P.22
Allsport P.22/23
P.24/25 Allsport
P.26/27 John Peters
P.28/29 Allsport
P.30/31 Allsport P.30
John Peters P.31
P.32/33 John Peters T/L P.32/33
Allsport B/L P.32 and B P.33
P.34/35 Empics T/R P.34 and B/L P.34
Allsport P.35
P.36/37 Empics P.36/37 (repeated from P.34/35)
P.38/39 Popperfoto/Reuters B/L P.38
John Peters P.39
P.40/41 Empics B P.40
John Peters
P.42/43 John Peters B P.42 and B P.43

Allsport T P.43
P.44/45 Allsport M P.44 and B P.45
Empics T P.44
John Peters B P.44
News International T. P.45
P.46/47 Allsport P.46
John Peters

The publishers would like to thank the following people for their help with this book:
Floyd Sayers for design assistance, John Peters and family for help with photographs, Belinda Ellington for technical support, Jon Somerscales (aged 10) for reading the text, Wilstead Lower School, Sam Izzard, Kim Hide, Helen and Kevin Butler.
The author would like to thank Esther McAuliffe and Justyn Barnes.